Complicity
Tom Sastry

smith|doorstop

Published 2016 by
smith|doorstop Books
The Poetry Business
Bank Street Arts
32-40 Bank Street
Sheffield S1 2DS

ISBN 978-1-910367-70-4

Designed and Typeset by Utter
Printed by Biddles Books

Acknowledgements

The willingness of poets to help improve the poems of others is
extraordinary. Every poem here has benefitted. Thanks to Jo Bell, Norman
Hadley and the 52 community; to Gram Davies and the Critical Bathtub;
to Jeremy Toombs and the Arts House open mic community and to
everyone I met at Ty Newydd.

'Thirty-two lines on loss' and 'Complicity' previously appeared in the
anthology *The Very Best of 52* (Nine Arches, 2015).

'The Office' appeared on *Ink, Sweat and Tears,* 'An Ordinary Day' on
The Fat Damsel

'A man begins to realise his failure as a husband whilst visiting the museum
of epiphanies with his soon-to-be-ex-wife' was highly commended in the
2006 Bare Fiction Poetry Prize and is due to be published on the Bare
Fiction website in May 2016.

smith|doorstop Books are a member of Inpress:
www.inpressbooks.co.uk. Distributed by Central Books Ltd.,
99 Wallis Road, London E9 5LN

The Poetry Business gratefully acknowledges the support
of Arts Council England.

Supported by
ARTS COUNCIL
ENGLAND

Contents

to Carly, Bethan and Elizabeth for my life as I now have it.

Waking

I dreamt that we were older. It didn't matter at all.
I was deaf and my balance was poor.
I couldn't smell the flowers. The warm grass
brought me out in hives. Your skin
was patterned. I loved it so much.
I proved it with kisses.
Our voices quavered but when they found clear notes
we felt the magic of it. There was nothing
to be coy about. Sometimes
we broke off, laughing because something ached.
We spent so much time in each other's eyes
that I learnt your face
properly. I named a new sense
and it swallowed the other five:
the sense of you, overwhelming everything.

I wake to the curl of you, the rise of breath.
Everything is paused.
At the window, there is proof of morning
but even now, the alarms are quiet.
You're asleep, or pretending.
You are peaceful and hot. My hair
crunches into you and you turn
as if you had been waiting.
I hope we will be slow.

Goldilocks

Everyone loved the wild girl. She meant
what we wanted her to mean. She cartwheeled
out of the forest like a ribbon, dirt on the bones
of her face; she screamed and bit, then washed
and smiled and played the piano. She said

that in the house a mile from the track
there were bears. She said the bears lived
in a house of secrets a mile off the track.
She said she ran from the house, and still wakes
in the night, trembling. There are bears in her sleep.

So we walked, a long line of women and men,
reporters and dogs, into the night of the wild girl
with our axes and our noses and our lifetime's rage.
We walked into the forest with our questions
looking for the house a mile from the track

where the bears live. We found the sun sliding down
the roof; we found the blinds down. What more proof
could there be? A hero struck the door
with the handle of his axe. Silence. His strong voice said
We are the people. It was all done well. We knew

the bears had the advantage. We couldn't see them
so we fell upon the house, all as one. No-one said
Charge! We were singing. We were parts
of a body that adored itself: because we were frightened
we loved each other, without realising.

We never found the bears but there were bones
in the ash we left: the skull of a child we were too late
to save; charred pieces of a man, perhaps
a woman too. Now, on Sundays, we ride our boots
back out into the wild girl's night. The hunt goes on.

I was talking with my marvellous man-friend

about our girlfriends with their friends and how it looks
so good the way they laugh together, like a dance you could
learn but not well; and how it's hard sometimes to believe
you could be worthy of time they could spend laughing like that

when I noticed he wasn't talking back. He had a kind of
yes-I've-thought-that-not exactly-that-but-close-enough
look, so I stopped looking for the mercy of regular trips
to the bar and the toilet and looked at him instead. He said that no-one

tells you how friendship is a mystery, like love, because that would be
to admit that the universe never promised us friends
but sometimes it's a thing you need to say out loud.
So I said yes, it was a mystery, how he was reflecting light

like a seventies space-funk tin-foil pearly king. What light was there
to reflect? It couldn't come from us, because we're extraverts
and our best enemies say we can only drain light from them.
Is it possible that our best enemies are wrong?

Sunday morning

He fell from my roof, hitting the path
with a sound which, if you knew at the time
what it meant,

would seem far too ordinary.
It didn't sound like bone, or skin or life
or anything more

than weight, dropped. He had been taking
MDMA, my neighbour said. He was a friend.
He was moving,

groaning; his eyes were red crescents.
His skin was bad. He had psoriasis.
No-one knew first aid.

Eventually, they took him away. The paramedic
said sorry, but it wasn't my body or her fault.
There was no blood.

Thirty-two lines on loss

Everywhere, they are selling:
the sun in orange juice; the sex
in perfume; thirty pence from a box
of fishfingers, tasting of sea. I lost

my glasses. I left them on the table
in the café because I was tired
of looking at billboards and wanted some thoughts
of my own and because I liked the fog of it

but when I went to leave, they were gone.
It was Sunday and the opticians
were closed. I soon realised that the world
is full of monsters travelling too fast.

One of these is time. I spent a lot of time sitting that day.
I drank a lot of coffee because that is what I do
when I sit. Perhaps I drank too much. I
did a lot of thinking and I wanted it

to last longer. But the sun set
and the sun rose and I called in sick
and got some new glasses. They filmed me
in the frames. I looked like a total dick

staring straight ahead like the world's
toothiest convict. You always do.
You accept it. They said it would take an hour
to make them up, so I went out

into the fog and found a café. I just killed time and
checked my phone but when I went to go
I couldn't get up. My body was a sandbag.
I cried like a doll. I must have really hated the idea

of functioning again. I hated it so much.
I hated it so much that for a moment
the surprise of how much I hated it
stopped everything, even the hate.

Red Pepper

A heart with four chambers
a heart with a hollow crack
a heart sliced into parentheses
a heart with its pith trimmed
a heart with its seeds binned
a red red red heart.

If my grandmother had had balls

she would have been a juggler
and joined the circus
where she would have learnt
how to eat fire
and not get burnt.

Instead, she kept house
with the violence
of a perfectionist
and left bruises
and is not missed.

Difference

Your lover remembers things differently. She says it was still autumn
there were green leaves on the ground, the light was milky-long

and she had already told you, so there was no mystery about what
she would say. And she says you were falling over

trying not to get your feet wet and that's how you pulled her
into the biggest puddle in the world. In a way, it was easy for her,

with the shock borne, shoes ruined, nothing more to fear.
Why not crash through, with furious limbs, shouting *What*

the fuck, what the fucking fuck? But you – you had to swamp in after her,
chilling your toes. There are leaves in your version too

but they are brittle white. You remember a burnt sugar crust
of ice on filthy water. But you did it! Even though you hated

the ruin of comfort, the fact that you would
never be safe and dry again, you did it! You ran

through the puddle because the answer might be you, and only stopped
when you were close enough to reach for her. Then you both

stood, sunk to the calves with spattered cheeks and kissed. Of course,
she remembers it differently. Not just that day. Everything.

A man begins to understand his failure as a husband whilst visiting The Museum of Epiphanies with his soon to be ex-wife

This exhibition will change your life
but for how long? It's boring –
the clamour for illusions, the clatter
of falling scales. Just past the turnstile

a wax girl sees a statue cry. She realises
that people prefer signs
to the thing signed for, that symbols
enlarge themselves by eating human

hearts. Your fences go up, come down.
Gurus prospect your emptiness.
There must be more than this, you cry.
The spirit enters you, the new age begins –

it is everything today is not.
We hide its promises behind our backs
in balled fists. You pick the left –
it's empty. The right is too

but just out of reach is a jar of the sixpences
on which the world once turned.
In the Gift Shop they sell magnets
to hold pictures to the fridge of your memory

whilst above you, and underwater,
a man realises that love happened
without him. This tea-towel says *Sorry*.
Let me buy it for you.

Magwen

The girl lives on a ship.
The ship is drifting from one story to the next.
The sea is her country. It is trying to eat her.

She is famous for her beautiful hair.
It is the pride of the ship. Everyone talks about it.
She hates that.
People touch it as if it was theirs.

They call her lucky.
They force limes into her mouth.
Otherwise, she lives on stale biscuit.

She is not scared of the sea.
She is scared of spiders.

A spider lives in her hair. The spider's name is Magwen.
Magwen loves the girl because she is warm.
The girl screams for days.

Cut off my hair! she screams.
Eventually they do. They keep her hair and throw her in the hold.
Magwen brings her flies to eat and spins her new hair.

When they have enough hair, they will make sails for the ship.

Cut off my hair! she screams.
Eventually they do. They keep her hair and throw her in the hold.
Magwen brings her flies to eat and spins her new hair.

Soon they will have enough hair to make sails for the ship.

Cut off my hair! she screams.
Eventually they do. They keep her hair and throw her in the hold.

They have enough hair.

The girl washes her head in vinegar. Magwen screams.

Land! she screams.

Magwen dies.

There is a terrible storm.
Men catch on the sails like flies on a web.
The sea-tongue licks the salt from its lip.
The girl vomits spiders.
There is no moral.

I imagine my white grandmother as a colonist stranded by the retreat of the Empire

She puts the force of her arm into each stitch.
She can't make cloth indestructible.
She makes it to resist.
She can't make it perfect.
She makes so the heart finds patterns.
If the savages come, they will see things
she has made. It will shame them,
even if they don't know it.

She governs six souls. They hate her.
She needs their work. Where they rest
bowls gape, plants thirst and tiles come loose;
wood wants wax; and sliver, polish;
bees flee and fires die –
so she spares no-one.
Voices rise, she quells them;
nails are driven and metal splashed.

She is the house.
Where she stands, there is order.
She stands against convenience;
against the changing certainties of men.
She is the guiding thought,
the will, the eye; the mouth of the day
that must be fed with work.
She will stay here. Hands will tend to her,

whatever their wish. She will kill if need be,
as she did when the soldiers came
and the weave was picked.
There was not a thing they did not do.
What they took, they took.
She gave them nothing.
She will hear no talk of freedom.
There is no such thing.

The Laundrette

She's the one who never calls me anything.
She tells them to go easy
even though I'm a provocation
still in my suit and drunk as them
but not away with it and scrubbed clean.

I don't give her the time.
I can see the remnants of her
like she's someone and no more than that.
But I have buttons to fasten and things to smoke
which I never share but sometimes

I give her the whole pouch and ask her children's names.
They're different each time.
I'm glad. She's hiding from me too
so we're quits.
She'll yell at the others

and walk right in as if she's allowed.
She'll sleep in the warm and buy her early
morning drink from the bearded guy who sells it
in soft drink bottles from a laundry bag
and wouldn't even acknowledge me

the time I asked,
just to see what it smelt like.
The laundrette opens eight to eleven.
There's a sign up. They want someone
to work an hour in the morning

opening up, and an hour at night,
throwing out the drinkers
until they don't come back.
Minimum wage? That's what it says:
Minimum Wage, question mark.

The Office

Keyboards slork and chirrup their way
through diets of words. The striped cough of the printer
punctuates the settling of sludge-mugs on the
woodskim tops. Everything has its
secret grammar. Voices skit and burr
on phatic tides; the cobbler's sigh imprints
the damped floor and a phone makes the sound

of a bird. I don't know which one. We do not have names
for birds in here. You can bring the name of a bird
in from outside, if you like. You can bring its call
on your ringtone, you can bring
the possibility of a bird. You can bring it on the chance
of a call from your letting agent or lover.
It can trill in your pocket.

Red

You're dead! You're dead! You're dead!
I got him! He's dead!

I'm not dead! I'm not dead!
He missed! I'm not dead!

Red means dead. The juice from
a beetroot slice

smuggled from the lunch hall
blooms on the shirt

my cursing mother bought.
I'm dead.

The museum of regret

You carry your takeaway cup
in the hand your daughter wanted.
The clock is too loud.

A woman sells strips of balsa wood.
The price is ten minutes.
You kneel with her, as Jesus would

then you draw pins from your knees
and make crosses
for the little shrines. Later,

you leave smeared prints on the glass
over the balled letters
and worn-out brakes.

It is Memory Day. They open the cabinets
to let the time in.
Something older than dust

jumps at the chance of an honest throat.
You ignore the cough.
Your office phone rings

and a woman cries on television. Two mannequins
turn their heads to face
each other, then turn away.

Someone calls last orders.
They switch off the ceiling fans
and let the air in –

you hear it singing
your mother's invitation, your lover's weekend
the last of the afternoon.

The suggested donation
is five pounds.

Jiggery Boomtish

As Jiggery Boomtish
he was indestructible
and therefore beyond compassion.

Once, we dropped him head first
from a crane into the orchestra pit
which triggered the fall of six thousand dominoes

spelling out the words *So What*. Two thousand people
laughed and someone shouted *Fuck off to hospital*
not because they cared but because they were drunk.

Only I knew that the extravagant distress
with which he greeted heckling
was real. Whilst incapable

of physical sensation
he compensated with language sense.
The first time we lay together, I touched his face.

What does it feel like? he said
And don't say a waterfall
I said it felt

like thin clouds fringing a heavy moon.
He said *How does the moon seem in your hand?*
and I said *Like laughter*. I know how this seems

but we were never lovers. Not the way I reckon things.
He discovered his necessity whilst I forgot mine.
So I made him curious about pain.

It was wrong
but I told myself he was selling
the ruin of his body

and had no gauge of it.
So I described sensations resembling
the grinding of metal

or the voice of Iain Duncan Smith.
He cowered and I felt ashamed.
After the last fall,

he asked me to describe
nothing.
What would it be like

to never imagine another touch?
Soon after, I left him, tubed and immobile
just so he would know.

Complicity

No-one knows where the clowns went.
Perhaps they found their own country.
Perhaps they were frightened.

Look –

there's a boy in Weston-Super-Mare
who says he saw, lined up on the mud at low tide,
small piles of braces, red wigs,
bellied pantaloons and oversized shoes.

The great marquees of England stand empty
and somewhere
a melancholy lion licks an abandoned red nose
whilst children fall over the guy ropes
with look-at-me smiles.

The politicians are explaining.
If they have left says the PM,
it was their choice.
I myself am the son of clowns.
We just wanted to disperse them
to prevent them from clustering together
in ghettoes.

It's not just him.
No-one says they feel guilty. There's just this

nostalgia. There are massive downloads
of classic bike horn and ukulele tunes.
New museums are planned.
The Commission on Nightmares
has proposed a new terror of badgers
but we all know it won't be the same.

We do our best to remember.

Last night, a group of us
sniffed trick roses on the bandstand
and wiped our dripping faces,
smudging our greasepaint smiles

Just words

I'm sorry. The waterfall was just words.
This is our bed. The birds never said
Join us. They wanted to
but they didn't know how. I'm sorry
that the tent sleeps in a Co-op bag for life
in the wardrobe. I'm sorry about the stars we can't see
and the mountain we didn't reach.

I'm sorry that it doesn't stop.
What if I turn it all off?
Listen. That's me,
stopping the hissing of the water
and padding back from the bathroom.
I brush past the shirts on the rail and click the main
light switch. The curtains whoosh

and the sound changes colour.
A pint of water lands on your table.
I'm tactile-careful in the dark, and slow.
Here I am. That's my voice.
I'm lifting off the roof. A hundred years shut
but it comes without a sigh. I'm stopping
the traffic and dimming the streetlights,

the ones in your head. I'm muting those
old arguments that go nowhere.
It doesn't matter if beautiful
things are called spiritual. Not to us.
We're bats, lovelier than birds.
We're talking in sonar.
We can't hear ourselves.

An ordinary day

All I know is the sun rising. The window faces east.
I am alive and alone to enjoy it.

Last night, I sensed a presence in the room.
The air thickened and I felt a weight on me.
I was too scared and too comfortable to move.

I don't believe in destiny
but I would like to be more accepting of things.

All I know is that the sun rises
whatever it is I expect to find.
There is nothing ordinary about it.

30 years

of smith|doorstop poets

Moniza Alvi, David Annwn, Simon Armitage, Jane Aspinall, Ann Atkinson, David Attwooll, Anne-Marie Austin, Sally Baker, Mike Barlow, Kate Bass, Paul Batchelor, Suzanne Batty, Zeina Hashem Beck, Chris Beckett, Peter Bennet, Catherine Benson, Gerard Benson, Paul Bentley, Sujata Bhatt, David Borrott, Nina Boyd, Maxwell Boyle, Sue Boyle, Carol Brierly, Susan Bright, Carole Bromley, Sue Butler, Peter Carpenter, James Caruth, Liz Cashdan, Dennis Casling, Julia Casterton, Claire Chapman, Debjani Chatterjee, Linda Chase, Geraldine Clarkson, Stephanie Conn, Stanley Cook, Bob Cooper, Jennifer Copley, Julia Copus, Rosaleen Croghan, Tim Cumming, Paula Cunningham, Simon Currie, Duncan Curry, Ann Dancy, Emma Danes, Peter Daniels, Peter Daniels Luczinski, Joyce Darke, Jonathan Davidson, Kwame Dawes, Owen Davis, Julia Deakin, Nichola Deane, Steve Dearden, Patricia Debney, Mike DiPlacido, Maura Dooley, Tim Dooley, Jane Draycott, Basil du Toit, Christy Ducker, Carol Ann Duffy, Sue Dymoke, Stephen Duncan, Suzannah Evans, Michael Farley, Rebecca Farmer, Nell Farrell, Catherine Fisher, Janet Fisher, Anna Fissler, Andrew Forster, Katherine Frost, Sam Gardiner, Adele Gèras, Sally Goldsmith, Yvonne Green, David Grubb, Harry Guest, Robert Hamberger, David Harmer, Sophie Hannah, John Harvey, Jo Haslam, Geoff Hattersley, Jeanette Hattersley, Selima Hill, John Hilton, Andrea Holland, Holly Hopkins, Sian Hughes, Keith Jafrate, Lesley Jefferies, Chris Jones, Mimi Khalvati, John Killick, Jenny King, Mary King, Stephen Knight, Judith Lal, John Lancaster, Peter Lane, Michael Laskey, Kim Lasky, Brenda Lealman, Tim Liardet, Katherine Lightfoot, Semyon Izrailevich Lipkin, John Lyons, Maitreyabandhu, Paul Matthews, Eleanor Maxted, John McAuliffe, Michael McCarthy, Rachel McCarthy, Patrick McGuinness, Kath McKay, Paul McLoughlin, Hugh McMillan, Ian McMillan, Allison McVety, Julie Mellor, Hilary Menos, Paul Mills, Hubert Moore, Kim Moore, David Morley, Sarah Morris, Blake Morrison, Paul Munden, Daljit Nagra, Dorothy Nimmo, Stephanie Norgate, Christopher North, Carita Nystrom, Sean O'Brien, Padraig O'Morain, Mark Pajak, Nigel Pantling, Alan Payne, Pascale Petit, Stuart Pickford, Ann Pilling, Jim Pollard, Wayne Price, Simon Rae, Irene Rawnsley, Ed Reiss, Neil Roberts, Marlynn Rosario, Padraig Rooney, Jane Routh, Peter Sansom, Tom Sastry, Michael Schmidt, Myra Schneider, Rosie Shepperd, Lemn Sissay, Felicity Skelton, Catherine Smith, Elspeth Smith, Joan Jobe Smith, Cherry Smytb, Martin Stannard, Pauline Stainer, Paul Stephenson, Mandy Sutter, Matthew Sweeney, Diana Syder, David Tait, Pam Thompson, Dennis Travis, Susan Utting, Stephen Waling, Martin Wiley, Tony Williams, Ben Wilkinson, Andrew Wilson, David Wilson, River Wolton, Sue Wood, Anna Woodford, Cliff Yates, Luke Samuel Yates

Laureate's Choice 2015 pamphlets
still available from the Poetry Business

David Borrott | Nichola Deane | Rachel McCarthy | Wayne Price

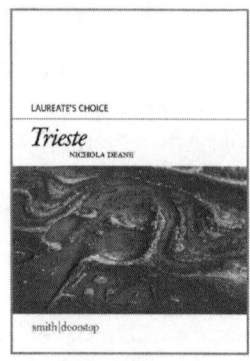

This is a varied but coherent collection, tender, imaginative and clear-eyed. – Carol Ann Duffy

A poet both sophisticated and lyrically charged who deploys imagery that is both precise and daring. – Carol Ann Duffy

Here are bold poems in a collection that is much more than the sum of its mesmerising parts.
                    – Carol Ann Duffy

A remarkable new poet who is intelligent, insightful, imaginative and utterly assured.
                    – Carol Ann Duffy

£7.50 each or all 4 for £20
www.poetrybusiness.co.uk

Thirty poems to celebrate thirty years of Poetry Business pamphlets

Founded in 1986 on an Enterprise Allowance, the Poetry Business was based for twenty years in a Victorian Arcade in Huddersfield, with poets Peter Sansom and Janet Fisher as co-directors. After Janet's retirement, the poet Ann Sansom took over as co-director and the business moved to its present offices in Bank Street Arts in Sheffield.

For all of those 30 years, we have been publishing pamphlets of one shape or another, starting with Simon Armitage's first published poems in *Human Geography*, right up until the present day with our Laureate's Choice pamphlets by four up-and-coming poets chosen by Carol Ann Duffy.

30 at thirty brings you thirty poems, one from each of the thirty years of the Poetry Business.

£5

www.poetrybusiness.co.uk